Fort Worth

a personal view

Fort Worth

a personal view

Photography by Phil Vinson

Foreword by Quentin McGown

TCU Press
Fort Worth, Texas

Library of Congress Cataloging-in-Publication

Vinson, Phil.
Fort Worth: a personal view / photography by Phil Vinson / foreword by Quentin McGown.
p. cm.
ISBN 978-0-87565-370-9 (alk. paper)
1. Fort Worth (Tex.)—Pictorial works.
2. Fort Worth (Tex.) – Buildings, structures, etc.—Pictorial works.
3. Historic buildings—Texas—Fort Worth—Pictorial works.
I. McGown, Quentin. II. Title

F394. F7V56 2008
976.4'5315060222—dc22 2007049767

TCU Press
P. O. Box 298300
Fort Worth, Texas 76129
817.257.7822
http://www.prs.tcu.edu
To order books: 800.826.8911

Designed by Whittington & Co., Austin, Texas
Printed in China by Everbest Printing Co. through Four Colour Imports, LTD., Louisville, Kentucky

For my wife, Rita.

Author's Note

"We photograph because we like what we see," wrote writer/photographer Robert Adams.

In my sixty years of living here, I've seen a lot to like in Fort Worth. The city's visual icons worked their way into my psyche from an early age. As a kid, I was fascinated by such sights as Mrs Baird's Bakery on Summit Avenue, historic Thistle Hill, the tower at the Will Rogers Complex, the Tarrant County Courthouse, the Texas Electric smokestacks, the art-deco design of the Texas & Pacific depot (where, as a child, I often waited for trains), and the Paddock Viaduct (my grandfather came from West Texas to work on the construction crew for the viaduct in 1914).

I started making photographs around the age of twelve. Yet it wasn't until adulthood that I began to rediscover the visual riches of my hometown. Once I started, I couldn't stop. I've spent the past four decades—mostly on weekend drives—seeking to recapture with my camera those early impressions, as well as many new subjects as the city grew and prospered.

Fort Worth has been well documented in photographs. A number of books feature the city's prominent landmarks. In this collection, I've tried to move beyond documentary records of the city's landmarks to present a more intimate, personal view of the city. I've often used close-ups and looked for dramatic light and compelling visual design in my pictures. I've found that getting in close to my subjects often reveals a universe of graphic possibilities that may not be obvious at a casual glance. I hope my approach and choice of subjects will show how I feel about this city and its environs:

sometimes joyful, sometimes sad, sometimes with my tongue stuck firmly in my cheek.

Most of these images represent the unmistakable heart and soul of Fort Worth for me. But because of my early years in Childress, I'm also drawn to rural or small-town subjects. Some of these pictures were made in small communities around North and West Texas, many of them places Fort Worth residents visit on weekend drives, such as Weatherford, Glen Rose, Granbury, Ponder, and Waxahachie.

I have great respect for subjects that have been around for decades, for they often acquire a certain dignity and nobility as they age. I've been aware of many old structures whose days may have been numbered, such as the Seventh Street Theater, and have made an effort to identify these places and make expressive photographs of them before they were demolished or altered beyond recognition.

The guiding principles of my photography have been derived from the f/64 school of photography, epitomized by photographers such as Edward Weston and Ansel Adams. I strive for maximum clarity and sharpness in my pictures. I've also been greatly influenced by dust bowl-era photographers such as Walker Evans and Dorothea Lange

This is my personal vision of Fort Worth. I'm grateful to be able to share it with you.

Phil Vinson
November 2007

Foreword

I'm from Fort Worth, and pretty proud about it. I cherish our city's history and think that we mostly do the right thing when it comes to facing tough issues and planning for the future. I love where we've been and can't wait to see where we're going. What is it about this city that makes me, and most folks I know, so ready to rush to its defense should someone make the mistake of slighting it? Or to feel good and right when we return home from a trip to some other place that's nice, but just not as nice as here? I admit to having a hard time articulating exactly what tugs at my heartstrings so tightly until Phil Vinson handed me a box of the photographs included in this book. What I struggled to put into words, he has captured on film. See if you don't agree with me.

Tucked into the covers of this remarkable book is a photograph of a long-vanished store in Arlington—Granny and Grandad's—where the welcoming sign over the front door read "Tired, Hungry, Thirsty, Lost…Stop Here." That bygone invitation caught Phil's eye more than thirty years ago, and I can't imagine a more appropriate subtitle for this collection of his personal views gathered over a lifetime of recording the texture and soul of Fort Worth and the territory surrounding us. This is no glossy Chamber of Commerce collection of souvenir city views. It's much better—and more emotional. With a journalist's focus, Phil captures the essence of the city that lies in the details we know are there but rarely slow down enough to ponder and appreciate.

When thirteen-year-old Phil received a dark-room kit, he knew he would follow in his newsman father's footsteps, recording the daily triumphs and tragedies of his adopted hometown. Nobody bought his pictures then, but a high school teacher told him he could, and should, write. He continued to carry his camera with him on news assignments, first with newspapers in Denton and Galveston, then for many years with the *Fort Worth Star-Telegram*. While his photography took a back seat to the writing, Phil never stopped seeing his stories through a focused lens. He left the news business in 1972 and returned to his first love, spending twenty-five years running his own commercial studio before closing shop and devoting his time to sharing his experiences with journalism students during nine years on the UTA faculty.

Phil told his students about his days as a cub reporter at the *Star-Telegram*, where a slightly older but by then veteran reporter named Jerry Flemmons advised him to "be succinct." From another teacher Phil heard, "when you think you're too close to something, get closer." Phil took both lessons to heart, certainly in his reporting but especially in his photography. In a time when we've become so used to seeing Fort Worth in big picture views, usually from behind our car windows, it's a treat—and a surprise—to stop long enough to focus on the details. Phil asks us to let him show us why he loves this place, and as he takes us on a personal tour, we discover that his city is our city

Much has changed here over the nearly forty-year span of these pictures. The lone silo of the old White Lake Dairy, once standing like a medieval battlement over the east Fort Worth hills, now sits hidden by development and concrete. Many of the weathered boards and faded signs have disappeared as the city has grown from the small town we'd still like it to be into the big city we sometimes struggle to recognize. But if I had to list those sights and scenes that daily remind me that my city is still here and alive, the list would be these images that Phil created—Dr. Saunders' panther heads on the Flatiron Building; the ingenious longhorn skulls on the old post office columns; the art deco geometry of the Blackstone Hotel; the chiseled elegance of the courthouse granite—each like an old companion requiring only a nod of recognition rooted in the comfortable knowledge that they are and will remain friends for life.

If you're "tired, hungry, thirsty, or lost" and need a reminder of just what it is that binds us to this place, "stop here" and gratefully accept Phil's comfort for the eyes and senses. He'll give you the smells and sounds of a spring morning at Inspiration Point, the still majesty of the Trinity River, and the wonder of a small bird peering into the eyes of an angel. The next time someone asks me why it is that I am so attached to my city, I won't have to struggle for words. I'll just hand them this book and watch them understand.

Quentin McGown
November 2007

Livestock Exchange, Fort Worth Stockyards, 2002

Railyards and Skyline from Hulen Street, 1975

Downtown from Northside Drive, 2005

Tarrant County Courthouse, 2003

Courthouse Dome, 2003

Tandy Center Reflections, 2002

Downtown, Winter, 2004

Downtown, Old and New, 2001

Courtyard by Marriott (Blackstone Hotel), 2005

Art Deco Detail, Texas & Pacific Building, 2001

Angel, Bass Performance Hall, 2003

Bass Hall Angel II, 2003

Civil Courts Building Angel, 2007

Panther Gargoyle, Flatiron Building, 2007

Main Post Office Sculpture, 2007

Longhorn Plaque, West Lancaster Bridge, 1978

Leddy's, North Main and Exchange Avenue, c. 1988

Cattle Drive, Stockyards, 2004

Longhorn, Near Crowley, Texas, c. 1982

Cattle Drive II – End of the Trail – Stockyards, 2004

Marie's Street Car Bar, Stockyards, c. 1986

Stanford Furniture, Stockyards, 2003

Gate Tower, Stockyards, c. 1983

Old Swift & Co. Logo, 2001

Staircase, Swift & Co. Ruins, c. 1983

Swift Staircase II, 1996

First Methodist Church, 2003

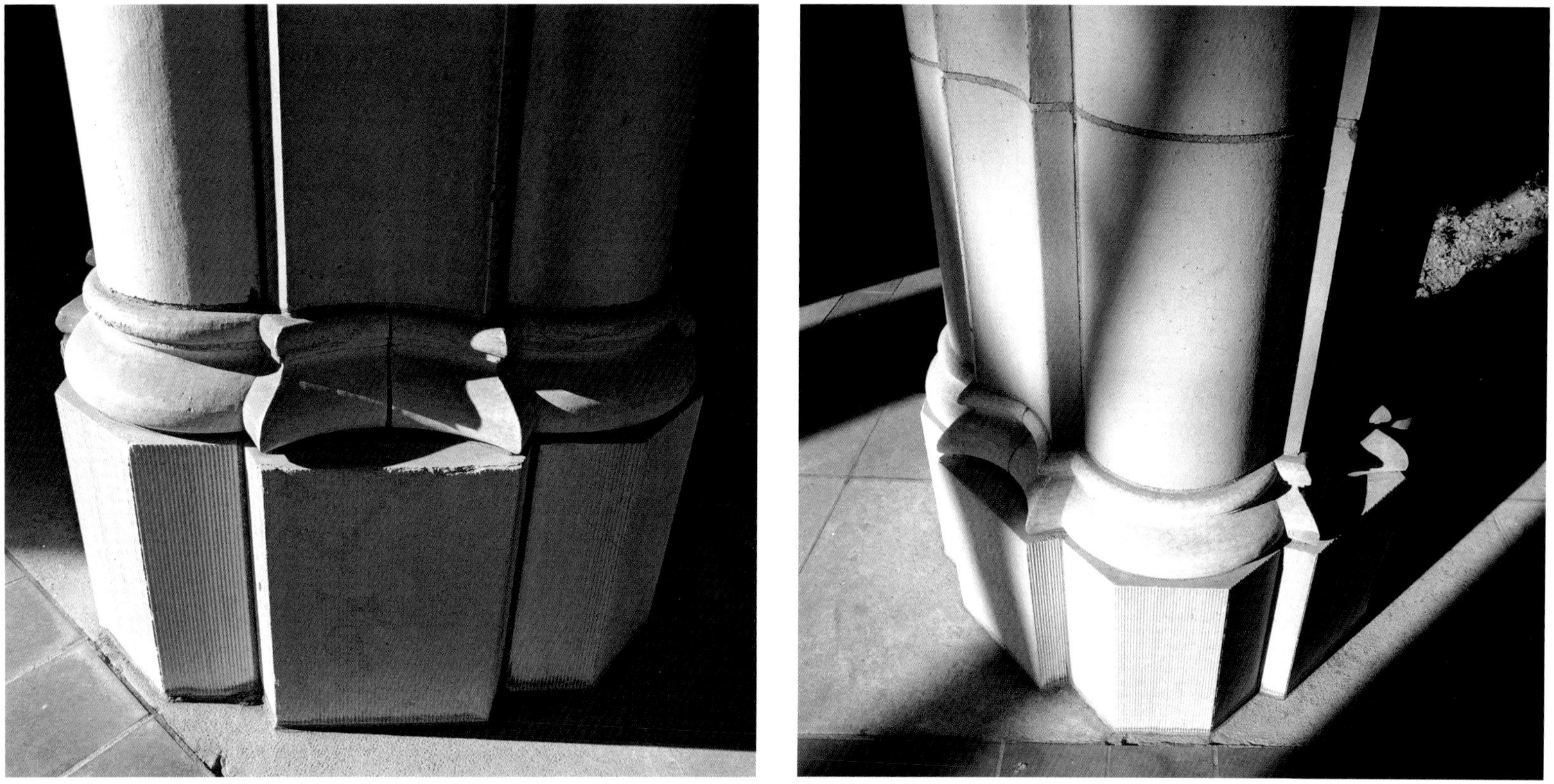

Two Views of a Pillar, First Methodist Church, c. 1988

Detail, Front Entrance, First Methodist Church, c. 1988

Pepper Logo, Chili's Restaurant, Downtown, 2005

Smokestacks, Texas Electric Service Co. Power Plant, c. 1987

Trinity River and Paddock Viaduct, 2003

West Seventh Street Viaduct, 2002

Santa Fe Depot, 2007

Antique Coke Machine, off Interstate 35, c. 1995

Famous Hamburgers, Downtown, c. 1985

Mexican Inn, Jacksboro Highway, 2003

Trinity River and Power Plant, Looking Northwest, 2001

Tarantula Train, Stockyards, 2001

Visiting Union Pacific Locomotive, T&P Station, c. 1987

Visiting Union Pacific Locomotive II, T & P Station, c. 1987

Marquee, Seventh Street Theater, 2002

Marquee II, Seventh Street Theater, 2002

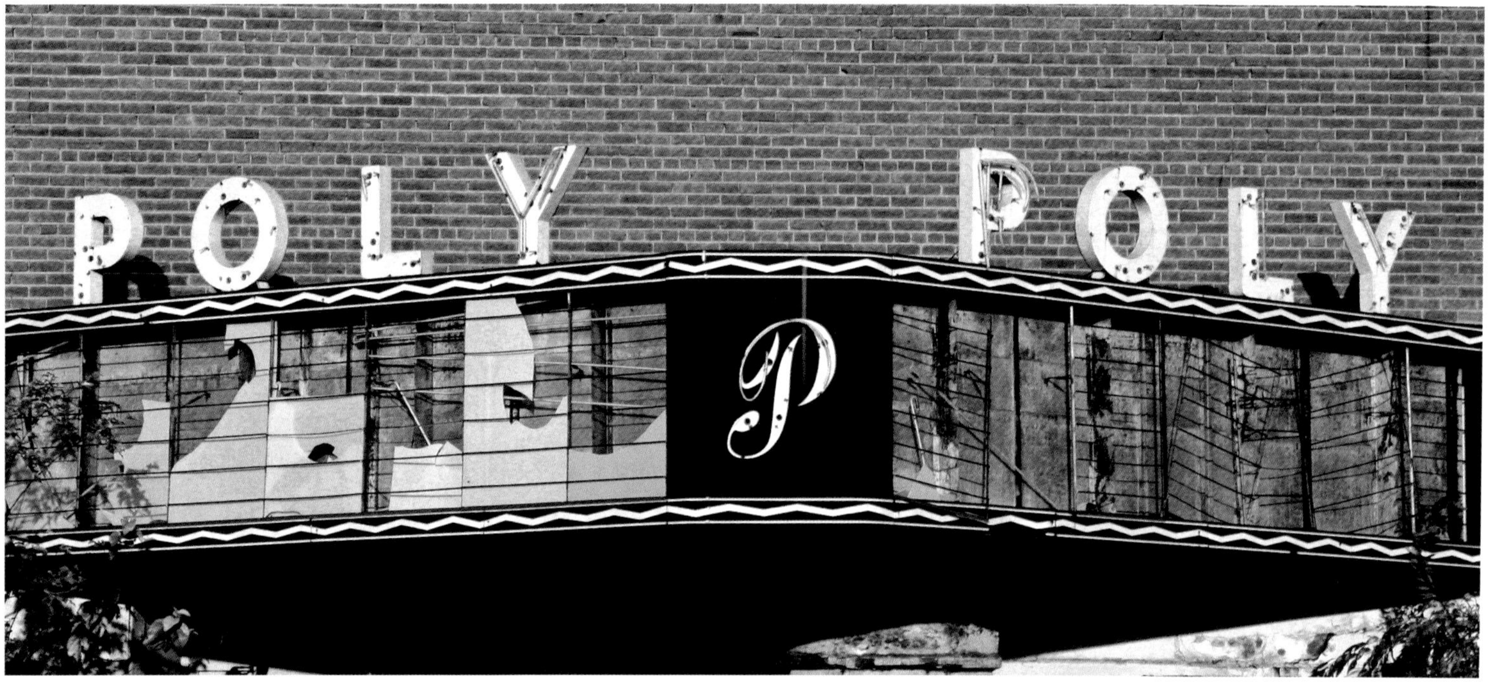

Marquee III, Poly Theater, 2007

Bowie Theater, c. 1984

Midway Drive In, West Texas, c. 1995

Empty Sign, Former Downtowner Motor Inn, 1998

Entrance Sign, Tindall Storage Warehouse, c. 1975

Clark's Grocery, Toronto Street, Sycamore Heights, 2003

Side Wall, Clark's Grocery, 2001

Yellow Window, Glen Rose, Texas, 2002

Abandoned Barber Shop, Magnolia Avenue, c. 1990

Barber Pole and Customer, Glen Rose, Texas, c. 1976

Noguchi Sculpture, Kimbell Art Museum, 2003

Roof Tiles, Fort Worth Japanese Garden, 2001

Sculpture, Buddhist Temple, Rendon, Texas, 2003

Rooftop, Fort Worth Japanese Garden, 1973

Buddha Statue and Neon, Rendon, Texas, 2003

James M. Moudy Building, TCU, c. 1983

Cotton Gin, Haslet, Texas, c. 1983

Granny & Grandad's, Arlington, Texas, c. 1974

Anguiano's Mexicatessen, Jacksboro Highway, 1972

Hood County Courthouse, Granbury, Texas, 2002

Ellis County Courthouse and Square, Waxahachie, Texas, c. 1985

Frog Sculpture, Botanic Garden Center, 2000

Interchange, Interstate 30 and Interstate 35, 2005

Antique Doll, Granbury, Texas, 2004

Steppingstone with Chinese Pictograph, After Rain, 1998

Sculptures and Sky, Amon Carter Museum, 2003

Hay Bales, Granbury, Texas, c. 1990

Grave Marker, Pioneer's Rest Cemetery, 2003

Grave Marker, Pioneer's Rest Cemetery, 1973

Grave Marker near Newark, Texas, c. 1975

Antique Interurban Car, 2004

Fire Station, Thurber, Texas, c. 1975

Rolls-Royce, Ponder, Texas, c. 1990

St. Patrick's Cathedral, c. 1986

Methodist Church, Roanoke, Texas, c. 1987

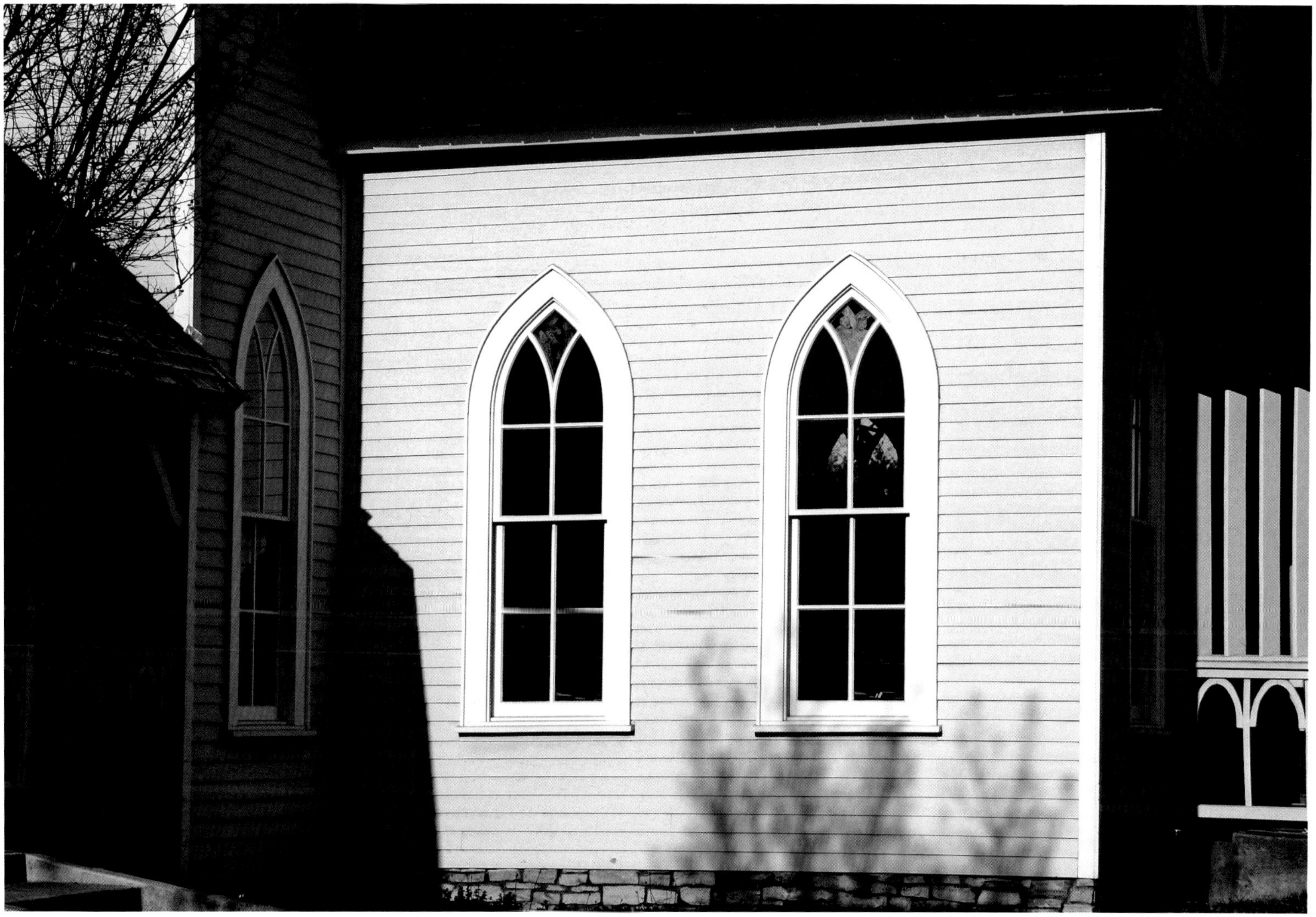

Christ the King Episcopal Church, 2006

Old White Church, West Cannon Street, 2002

Leaning White Church, Near Mansfield, Texas, c. 1990

Marty Leonard Chapel, Lena Pope Home, 2006 (Altered in Photoshop)

Silo and Clouds, Oakland Boulevard, 1960

Thunderhead and White Lake, c. 1977

Fort Worth National Bank/Bank One, 1973

Fort Worth National Bank Reflections, c. 1978

Robert Carr Chapel, TCU, 2002

First Leaves of Spring, Lake Worth, c. 1974

Trinity River, Foggy Day, c. 1997

Old Sinclair Station, South Main, c. 1984

Milk Can Mailbox, Acton, Texas, 1973

Collapsing Privy, Near Mansfield, Texas, c. 1990

Ponder Boot Co./Ponder State Bank, Ponder, Texas, c. 1990

Dressmaker's Dummy, Hereford, Texas, c. 1987

Hotel Sign, Graford, Texas, c. 1975

Depot, Meridian, Texas, 1973

Paddock Viaduct, c. 1987

Pumpkins, Public Market, Weatherford, Texas, c .1995

Fort Worth Stock Exchange, c. 1984

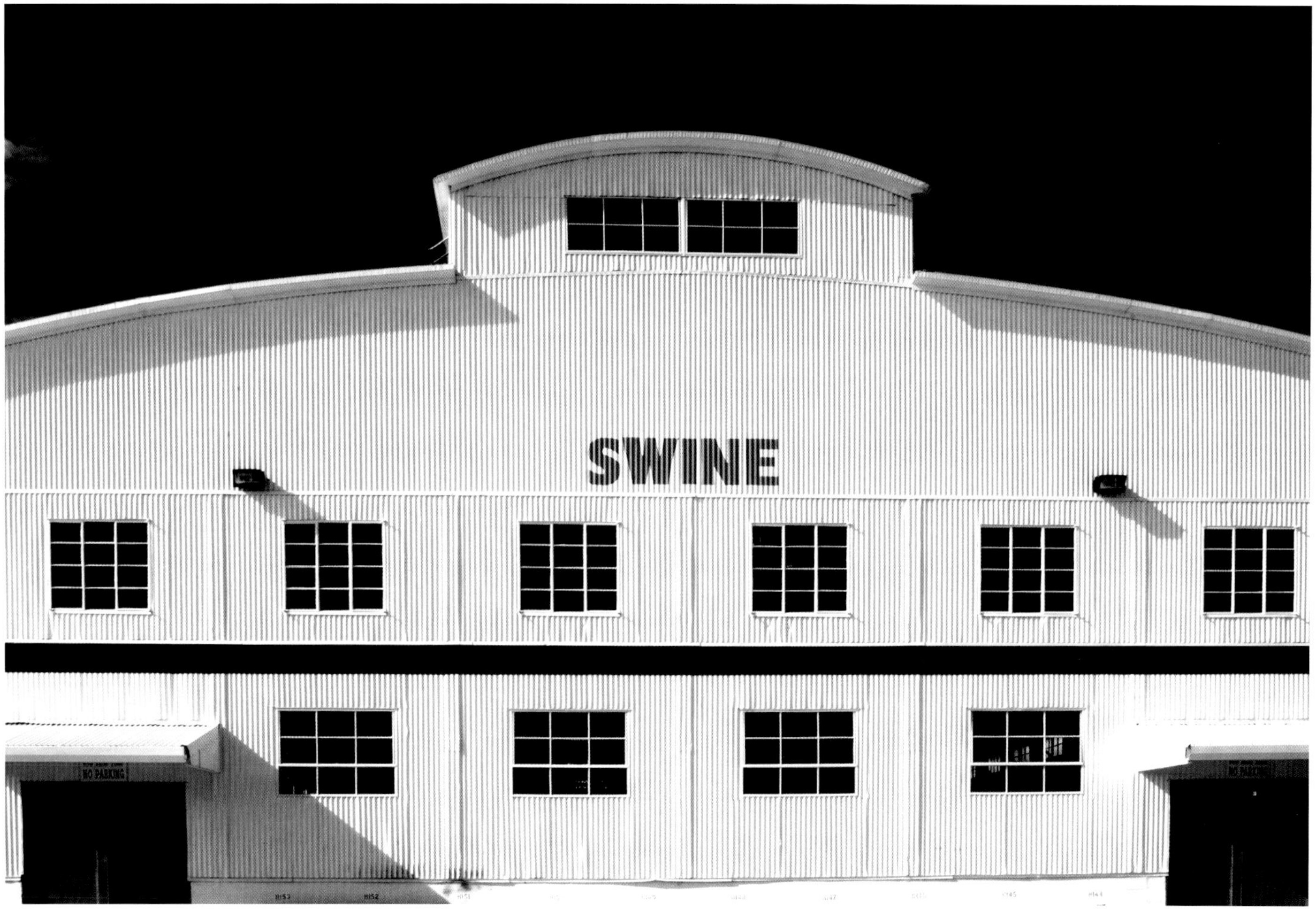

Livestock Barn, Will Rogers Memorial Center, 2003

Statue, Will Rogers and "Soapsuds," WRMC, c. 1985

Waiting Room, Amtrak Station/Santa Fe Depot, c. 1987

Peters Bros. Hats Sign, Downtown, 2002

Gables, Thistle Hill, Pennsylvania Avenue, 2002

Eddleman-McFarland House, Summit Avenue, 2002

Paddock Viaduct, Foggy Day, 1998

Lonesome Road, Denton County, c. 1989

Fort Worth Skyline, Sunset, c. 1976